GLEANINGS FROM THE MASTER'S TABLE

By

Joy U. Obialor-Egekwu

Foreword by HE Apostle Dr. Patience Oti

The following versions of the Holy Bible were consulted for this work - Authorized King James Version by Zondervan (2000), New Living Translation, 2015 by Tyndale House Foundation.

ISBN: 978-1-7332848-4-4

APPRECIATION

My deepest appreciation goes to the best mentor and motivator on planet earth - bar none - Her Excellency, Apostle Dr. Patience Ogechi Oti, whose 52-day challenge to the Tribe on August 13, 2023 spurred me to actualize this book. Thank You!

Mrs. Blessing "Inspire" Okwa, you are one of a kind. You challenged me in more ways than one. Thank you for not hesitating to handle the behind-the-scene details that made this publication a reality.

Dr. Chinedu, or should I say "Eagle Chinedu" as you are fondly known. It would have been next to impossible to have a decent material from a mass of unorganized manuscript, were it not for your masterful editorial skill. You possess a pair of "*eagle-eyes*" that can spot what is otherwise hidden from "*normal*" eyes and transform same into a masterpiece. Thank you for making this infant writer appear professional.

My Dear favorite pastor, Pastor Sam Eke, only eternity will reveal the impact your teachings, preachings, lectures, etc., have made on countless individuals over the years. In the meantime, let the record show that this writer is one person so greatly impacted. Those moments when I sat glued to my seat in rapt attention, listening to what God has to say through you, led to this *acorn* becoming an *oak*. Thank you. I am forever indebted to you.

"...What do you have that God hasn't given you? And if everything you have is from God, why boast as though it

were not a gift? I Corinthians 4:17 (NLT).

The Almighty God gave me every blessing I have received in my life. So, I return all glory and honor to my Lord and Savior, Jesus Christ, without whose help this book would not have materialized. Thank You Papa.

FOREWORD

Very often, gleams of light come in a few minutes, sleeplessness in a second perhaps; you must fix them. To entrust them to the relaxed brain is like writing on water; there is every chance that on the morrow there will be no slightest trace left of any happening. Antonin Sertillanges

Under this backdrop, this diligent scholar, Minister Joy Obialor-Egekwu, took copious notes at different meetings and events for years. According to Robert Boice, "taking notes allows you to engage with the material at a deeper level".

Having synthesized the notes, the author has come out with this succinct masterpiece - *Gleanings from the Master's Table*. As the name suggests, these are extracts, the best of the best. A cow drinks 4 to 4.5 liters of water per kilogram of milk it produces. This book cuts off the water and serves you pure milk. No fluff.

The book runs the full gamut, from presentations made by accomplished leaders to knowledge acquired by just living life. I picked up a copy of this book and could not stop reading until I completed the last page. Many memories came back; many decisions were taken for good.

I have shared Altars with this author on many platforms: Tribe Prayer Line, Sandy Cove Retreats, Shekina Ministries Bible School, Shut-Ins and Foreign Missions. I can boldly say that she is the real deal. I highly recommend this book. I pray that you will be blessed.

H.E. Apostle Dr. Patience Oti.

DEDICATION

To every pastor, teacher, minister, and preacher who ever committed and shared what they received from God, I dedicate this work. Also to every lecturer who ever taught a student from the pages of the sacred Scripture, and to every student that ever sat under the tutelage of a Bible teacher, I dedicate this work. To you who are holding this book of collections, I sincerely dedicate this work. To all the Egekwus and the Obialors, far and near, I dedicate this work.

And finally, to Ifeanyi and Chido, our amazing sons, for your thirsty readiness to absorb everything I glean, I lovingly dedicate this book.
Blessings!

INTRODUCTION

"As you enter the house of God, keep your ears open and your mouth shut" Ecclesiastes 5:1 (NLT).

A pair of open ears and a shut mouth allow one to keenly listen, learn and absorb. However, one of the proven ways to remember, review, and share what one has learned is to write down the "Aha moments." This is because, according to Her Excellency, Apostle Dr. Patience Ogechi Oti, "a short pencil is better than a long memory."

My "short pencil" is the tool that built "Gleanings from the Master's Table" and put it in the reader's hands today.

ENDORSEMENT

It is a privilege to endorse this book, "Gleanings from the Master's Table". As an avid reader, I know a good book when I see one. I highly recommend Minister Joy Egekwu's book. It is brief but loaded. This is the size this busy generation will love to read. You will glean so much on so many topics in very few hours.

Thank you, Minister Joy for giving us this gem.

Hon. Dr. Patience Oti (OAS)
President, Shekina Charities.

We've all been there. We come across a quote or statement that resonates so deeply with us, we scramble to find pen and paper to capture its essence. Some of us jot them down on random scraps, others in a journal, and sometimes even on the pages of a book we're reading. But how amazing is it that author Ms. Joy Egekwu has taken the time to gather these gems together for our reading pleasure? Not only that, but this compilation serves as a source of guidance, inspiration, and upliftment. If you're anything like me, you'll find yourself highlighting countless passages that speak directly to your soul. This remarkable work deserves to be cherished and kept close by for easy access, revisiting, referencing, and ongoing encouragement. Thank you, Ms. Joy Egekwu, for curating this invaluable collection.

Mrs. Okwa Blessing Ofem
Brand Strategist
www.blessinginspire.com

Readers make great leaders; writers make greater and more enduring leaders. This is because the impact of writers outlives them. The concept of using a short pencil rather than relying on a long memory teaches that whatever is written becomes a reference point, not just for the current generation but for posterity. *Gleanings From the Master's Table* is made possible because the author, Minister Joy Obialor-Egekwu, aptly ran with the vision of keeping a pencil (and invariably a jotter) close by to document, no matter how insignificant, to absorb and act upon information that comes our way. These simple tools of pen and jotter make a huge difference for today and for tomorrow. Habakkuk 2:2 exhorts us to "Write down the vision and make it plain, that he may run that reads it."
If you get into the habit of jotting down stuff, (try this during phone conversations), you will be pleasantly amazed at how much power you can exert over your time, human and material resources. Thank you, Minister Egekwu for a collection of transcripts whose hour has arrived.

Eagle (Dr.) Chinedu Christie Nnamah Okoye, JP

To know is to live, as such I approach every opportunity to learn with much enthusiasm. I read this book with that avidity and every sentence in the book fueled my longing and at the end there were no disappointments.
I gleaned this book with both my eyes and ears open and was left mouth agape from deep truths communicated. The truths shared are very relevant for the today Christian who

wants to excel in life and please His Maker.
I congratulate Minister Joy Obialor-Egekwu for this giant stride while praying for more of this kind of accomplishment.
I strongly recommend this book, Gleanings from the Master's Table. It is a must read for everyone who desires a deeper fellowship with God and victory in all spheres of life.

Pastor Sam Eke.

TABLE OF CONTENT

THE FLASH

The day was Wednesday, September 28, 2022. Sitting in my office, I prepared for my annual one-on-one meeting with the director of my establishment to discuss the management's evaluation of my 2022 performance. As was my custom, I took a notepad along to jot down key points from the discussion. As I picked up the jotter, my eyes caught this phrase on the cover of my notepad: "*There is no tool for development more effective than the empowerment of women.*"

However, I think there is more to the empowerment of the female specie that determines the effectiveness of development, and that factor is the *God Factor*. Regardless, I love the quote, and I felt in my heart that more of such quotes were needed to motivate people at various times.

I allowed myself to briefly reflect on all the priceless quotes I had gathered through the years of personal readings, teachings by others, at conferences, retreats, professional studies, and the like. Over the years, I had amassed priceless nuggets that I revisit from time to time. I find them very refreshing and instructional. They have ministered and continue to minister to me at various phases of my life. That was when it "flashed" through my mind: "Why don't you condense these precious nuggets into a printable format and share with others?" Wow! It sounded like an awesome idea. Although I was convinced that this was nothing short of a "God-idea", I wondered how and when I could find the time to take on such a daunting task.

In the end, I sat down, recorded my thoughts, and was determined to embark on the task at some point in the future.

As always, life and work never ceased to call. Consequently, these gleanings remained at the back burner of my mind, simmering...

THE BABY STEPS, AND THEN...

Despite my feeble attempts on several occasions to organize these gleanings into a printable format, "interruptions" never seemed scarce. Life, family, career, ministry, and travels made demands that I could not ignore. Demands and more demands chipped away at what time I had, and there was never "a good time" to sit down and organize these gleanings.

On August 13, 2023, the Tribe Prayerline, (a group of believers who meet daily on Zoom to read, study the scriptures, and pray from 4:30 am to 5:30 am EDT), read Nehemiah 6:15, *"So on October 2 the wall was finished—just fifty-two days after we had begun"* (NLT).

In exposing this scripture, the pioneer of the Tribe, our "one-of-a-kind" Prayerline Ministry, Apostle Dr. Patience Ogechi Oti, threw down the gauntlet to Tribe members. She challenged every Tribe member who had an uncompleted business to "Go finish your unfinished project in 52 days counting from August 13, 2023!" That was my personal wake-up call! I picked up that gauntlet and ran without looking back. Fifty-one days later, (October 3, 2023), I was holding the manuscript of "Gleanings from the Master's Table." Phew! Time to exhale!

THE INVITATION

I penned these gleanings with fervent prayers. I urge you, dear reader, to enjoy them as much as I do. Allow them to minister to you as they did and continue to minister to me. Revisit them often for inspiration. And as a proof of what they mean to you, share them with others.

Blessings!

GLEANINGS FROM SHUT-INS

(These gleanings were gathered from the various Tribe "Shut-ins" I attended in the past years.)

What is Prayer?

Prayer is an open door into the presence of God. It is an invitation for real people to express real needs to a listening, loving Father, and receive real, tangible answers from a gracious and loving God.

Believers pray so that God can do for them the things they cannot do for themselves. God is the Supreme ruler of the universe. He is able, willing, and ready to move heaven and earth to help His children. But when we, His children, feel self-satisfied, we lose the need to be God-satisfied.

My Father created all I needed before He brought me to earth. For that reason, I constantly grow from standing to outstanding as the Lord matures my eyes to see "my well of living waters". Whomever God makes the Bezalel of their time, becomes the carrier of blessings in their generation. So, we need to be careful to desire or attract only those things we truly need or want.

I have come to learn that it is better to die believing God, than to live not believing Him.

As a teachable child of God, my duty is to believe God's promises. God's task is to determine "how" to make His promises come true in my life.

- God has a million ways to deliver His miracles. It really does not matter the method He uses to do so. What matters is that He delivers.
- We know that gold is never found on the surface of the earth, but underneath.
- Never be limited by what you don't have. Whatever God has not given to you, you do not need and should not desire.
- I affirm that I am the seed of God's life sown into the ground of my generation.
- When God wants to prepare a people, He first makes them whole. Get into God's business of "whole".
- Since God has made me the mother of many nations, I will not die, but I will live and touch nations.
- My birth is God's idea. My salvation is God's idea. My winning soul is God's idea.
- My God is the God of "by this time tomorrow."
- Nothing can take away God's crown of glory from me.
- My head shall wear a crown. My head shall not be barren. My place will be a place of harmony.
- When God takes me on a walk, He takes me to dimensions and not levels.
- A man with a vision does not die until the message is delivered.
- When I catch the vision of heaven, everything earthly becomes dung.
- Sometimes the king in my life has to die for me to see the purpose of God.

Prayer: *Lord, do a new thing in my generation and include me in Your doing.*

WORDS TO REMEMBER

(These gleanings came from church teachings, exhortation as well as retreats, conferences, trainings, etc.)

- God sponsors His assignment. He does not bless our greed.
- God supplies grace for the race He wants us to run.
- No devil can take me out before my assignment is over/done.
- The weeds have nothing capable of killing the seed in God's garden.
- I am sustained by a higher economy because God ensures that His ambassadors are cared for.
- When there's a casting down, there's always a lifting up for God's children.
- Ambassadors are only protected when they are in their places of assignment. So be sure to follow God's purpose and not your preference.
- Favor is often released at the place of one's assignment. Therefore my ambition is subordinate to God's assignment.
- Don't come to the end of life and realize you only just existed! Leave your footprint in the sands of history.
- Nothing frustrates in old age than the realization that one did not take advantage of great opportunities but one had missed them all!
- It's a dangerous way of living when you limit your stay only in the midst of people who make you feel good.

- "Difference" is the seed that makes for success; don't let it intimidate you.
- When you pursue a God-given assignment, it will take you to places you never dreamt of.
- The love for pleasure gradually takes away our treasure. Stop the erosion!

Here are the characteristics of fire:

1) Fire consumes,
2) Fire purifies,
3) Fire comforts, and
4) Fire rekindles.

- If you begin to find pleasure in what used to grieve you, but it still grieves the Holy Spirit, check your "fire".
- If you can no longer speak out for Christ where you used to, check your "fire".
- If you no longer pray and study the Bible like you used to, check your "fire".
- If you no longer show compassion and accept people of low estate, check your "fire".
- If you once made Jesus a standard but now use other Christians to justify your weaknesses, check your "fire".

A believer that resists Godly disruptions will miss their life mission.

A prideful spirit will seldom accomplish anything for God.

A true disciple is not made overnight.

Abundance cannot happen in your life until the One who should control your life takes His place within you.

Any king surrounded by dishonest lips will be led astray.

Any strategy that does not come from God is bound to fail.

Anyone who runs away from the light goes to hide in the darkness.

Anything that comes from fear is of the devil.

Be careful not to kill your troop with "friendly fire".

Become a reference point of God's blessings to those around you.

Before you blame God, check to see if the blame arrow is pointed in your direction.

Beware! Complex combination of elements results in complication and the major source of complication is the devil.

Circumstances will never change Jesus.

Concentrate on doing the right things, and the wrong things will fade away.

Conspiracy will come to nothing because when the Lord is for us it matters not who is against us.

Determine to be incapable of doing nothing in God's Kingdom.

Discard excuses and embrace grace. I am what I am and will be what I will be through God's grace.

Do not invite a permanent problem into your life because of a temporary problem that comes to pass.

Do not perceive rejection when none is present.

Do not trifle with the name of Jesus. This is because when you call it in faith, it answers with miracles.

Do you know that once upon a time you were an "outsider"?

Don't agonize over things that you should hand over to God.

Don't be a house divided against itself, because unity is the foundation of divine visitation.

Don't be distracted from what God has told you – maintain a tunnel vision.

Don't go to church with your filters on.

Don't let what should belong to God end up in your house.

Don't tell God your experiences; tell Him your expectations, because those are what will not be cut off.

Don't use yourself to judge the healing power of God; use the finished work on Calvary.

Don't worry about the throng, press in and focus on the touch.

Every willful sin starts by believing the first lie.

Faith ignores the fact; it doesn't deny it.

Faith is a tool, a seed, and a weapon. It is the hand that reaches into the spiritual and pulls down miracles.

Favor produces favor, and for that reason I will enjoy God's goodness in the land of the living.

Fight on your knees, and fight till the end.

For every Elijah, there is a "woman of Zarephath", and for every Elisha, there is a "woman of Shunem".

Getting rid of old things brings in the new – evening gives way to morning and the father gives way to the son.

Go for joy and stay joyful. Guard your joy so your strength is not tampered with.

God is a God of new things, and I am a product of mercy.

God loves us just as we are, but loves us too much to leave us that way.

God's agenda is more rewarding than anything I can come up with.
God's grace is the only reason the persecutor of the Church can become the leader of the Church.
Grace can wipe away my past and rewrite my future.
Grace invites me back into the ship.
Grace is my tailwind. It is the wind beneath my wings, lifting me to heights unimaginable.
Grace is the only elevator that takes me to high levels without exhausting my energy.
Grace turns "noisemakers" to "news-makers."
Growth cannot be attained when you stay outside of your God-assigned growth area.
Hope that is in God's hands is indestructible.
How can God trust you if He doesn't know you?
I am a letter written by God and sent to my family, my society, and the world.
I am no longer in my cocoon, for God has released me; henceforth, I will spread my wings and fly.
I am who I am because of Whose I am.
I will forget the past, so that I am not kept from the future.
If God doesn't trust me in the winter season, He can't trust me in the spring season. So, I must remain faithful when it seems as if nothing is happening.
If you desire to be effective, find God's purpose and pursue it relentlessly.
If you want freedom, you must roll away the stone.

If you want to provoke a turn-around, get desperate.

If you're not informed, you're deformed. So, study, prepare, and wait for elevation.

Ignorance is more dangerous than the devil. Avoid it.

Inability to praise God is pride in disguise.

It is a rewarding habit, to consistently serve God with joy and excellence.

It is a tragedy to live outside of God's presence; because outside his presence are frustration and depression.

It is daydreaming to believe you can accomplish a goal you did not set.

It is impossible to be bored within the will of God.

It is impossible to be emotionally healthy outside of Jesus.

It is never too late to become what you could have become.

It's impossible to fall in love with a God you don't know. Get to know Him!

Jesus died a shameful death so that I will never suffer shame.

Jesus died of a broken heart so that my heart can be made whole.

Just when everyone thinks it's over, grace steps in.

Learn to step up and be counted; don't cover up with regrets, pain and fear.

Men may delay one's blessings from God, but they can never stop it.

My eyes are set forward, because if I drive looking in the rearview mirror, a crash will be inevitable.

My past disqualifies me, but God's grace qualifies me. The God who calls me fully equips me.

Never hoard your compliments; give them out freely and frequently.

Never stand and gaze at how far you've come, focus on terrains yet unconquered.

No matter how beautiful a flower looks, once it is cut off the branch, it dies.

No matter where I've been, the Spirit that quickens can revive me.

No one will ever discover new territories, as long as their boat is anchored ashore.

No place is too dark for Jesus to be victorious.

No prayer, No victory! Know prayer, Know victory!

Nothing in success is more important than the favor of God.

Nothing will get done if everyone becomes a spectator.

Once you're too full of yourself, you'll stop thirsting for God.

Only when you need something will you get something.

Operate in the offensive and the devil will lose the battle.

Operate in the defensive and you will lose.

Our God does not compensate laziness.

Parrots talk too much but can't fly; eagles keep silent but soar to great heights.

Ponder this! Where will you go when you sense revival breaking out around you?

Prayer does not substitute thinking; it makes a demand on God's character and identity; it partners with God for His promises.

Prayer increases the awareness of God, clarifies God's will and helps bring down strongholds.

Prayer is primarily spending time with Jesus; get into the habit.
Prosperity is a person and His name is Christ.
Relying on God's grace makes everything work better.
Remember, only a dead grain bears fruit.
Remember, problems do expire. And once they do, victory is on the way.
Resist from pushing a gospel that does not transform lives. So, go only when you've received the power.
Sitting and being taught at the feet of Jesus is one of the believers' most powerful weapons.
Stay rooted, don't let people talk you out of your blessings, and don't talk yourself out either.
Stop asking what God will give you; start asking what you will do for God.
Stop hiding; come out and challenge whatever is challenging you.
The authority we have in Christ is able to remove any mountain we encounter.
The greater your level of growth in the Lord, the greater the devil that is sent to buffet you.
The Law of Vision: It's a crime to wake up daily with no vision because our God is a God of "new".
The Lord will give me a reason to sing and will use me to showcase His power.
The more like Christ I am the better person I become.
The only way to abide in God is to abide in Jesus.
The power of God heals, and the love of God transforms and delivers. We have both!

The strongest network is prayer; it can't be overwhelmed, hacked or brought down.

The trees planted by God have the tendency to spread their branches over the wall.

There are no lone rangers in God's kingdom.

There's greatness in serving; so if you can serve, you can be great.

There's more ahead of you than what's behind you.

There's no pit so deep that God's love is not deeper than.

There's nothing the power of God cannot do; for there's no limit to God's power.

Those who desire to "hear" and "see" must learn to remain in God's presence.

Three things that amaze the angels: 1) Jesus became human; 2) Jesus died for me; 3) Jesus lives inside of me.

To open a new chapter, one must close the old chapter; so forget what is behind and reach for what's ahead.

Try as we may, no one can kill that which cannot die.

Unless the Lord has all of you, He really has none of you.

Until you become intentional, no good thing will happen.

Watch what you say, and don't corrupt your blessings with your words; words are critical and determine your destiny.

We are Christ's church, and we belong to each other, just as much as we belong to God.

We will do greater works, for it is Jesus' commitment to answer our prayers.

What can't you give up to follow Jesus?

What you don't confront, you cannot change.

Whatever sits on the throne of your heart controls your every action.
Whatever tries to hold me back will have Jehovah to contend with.
When a Greater than Moses shows up, all curses are broken.
When God believes in me I can get the job done.
When God calls something, that is what it becomes.
When God has clearly given you instructions, don't be swayed by man's advice.
When God is in the burning bush, it won't get consumed.
When God moves, He does so for His glory; He distinguishes His children from the crowd.
When God sees a bag full of holes, He does not pour His blessings into it.
When God's name is on the line, He answers.
When I build capacity, God performs and deposits in me as much as I can handle.
When labor pain intensifies don't give up, because your baby is about to be delivered.
When one trusts God for greater things, they happen; learn to trust Him for greater things.
When something leaves your hand for God, something leaves God's hand for you.
When the King loves you, it doesn't matter who doesn't.
When the river flows, whoever jumps in is made whole.
When there's a capacity problem, check your side, because the problem is never on God's side.
When we don't realize that God is here", we miss our

opportunity.

When you are spiritually desperate, you will encounter the Lord.

When you are unable to see face-to-face, you cannot reason heart-to-heart.

When you change what you've always done, newness will emerge.

Whenever we are willing, God shows Himself as being able.

Wherever I arrive, Jesus is there.

Whether I touch God, or God touches me, I will experience the same result.

Worshipping idols is useless and a waste of precious time.

You can only carry “you” so far; you need God's hand to carry you through.

You can tell a tree by looking at the fruit.

You have no idea how impactful encouragement can be until you give it out.

You may not have enough, but the bottle of oil will not cease neither will the barrel of flour be exhausted.

Your attitude will determine your altitude.

Your mouth is the most potent part of your body; use it wisely.

Your perspective of Christ will determine your level of prayer.

GLEANINGS FROM STUDIES

(These gleanings were gathered during my various times of studies for devotions, exhortations and teachings)

"Me", "Myself" and "I" do not equal love.
A soul without hope is dead.
All Believers are called to serve, not to be served – get on board.
As a believer, doing nothing to help is not an option.
Be careful what you are building; God's kingdom is the only thing that will last forever.
Be careful who has your ears, their influence is unimaginable.
Beware! Sodom and Gomorrah exhibited pride, excessiveness, prosperity-induced laziness, idleness, selfishness, arrogance, in addition to immorality.
Do not waver in your faith; if you stay focused, Jesus will stop for you.
Don't let fear imprison you from maximizing your potentials.
Don't let your feelings dictate your response or action.
Don't let your prayers become blank bullets; load your heart with faith.
Every time the devil plans a burial, God lowers a ladder for climbing out of the grave.
Focus on the bigger picture and resist the urge to settle for crumbs; we serve a protocol-breaking God.
God knows how to block every spirit of mutations in my life.
Godliness trumps everything else.

Guardrails do not guarantee success in Godly living; only God does.

Have the courage to stand for something even if you have to stand alone.

Home is wherever the Father, the Son and the Holy Spirit are.

How you care for others is how your greatness is measured.

I see the fact, but I believe the Truth.

If we have any idea of God's plans for us, we will hurry up and get there.

If you desire to implement practical Christian living, find the poor and help them out.

If you don't contend for what has been given you, the devil will steal it.

Integration happens when God's light infiltrates our dark world and transforms us into God's children.

My level of grace can never be withstood by any demonic activity.

Never forget what God has done; they are faith-building blocks.

Nothing significant can be built apart from God as the foundation.

Our visions cannot diminish that of anyone else's.

People will serve the God I serve when they see God's evidence in my life.

Prodigal children cannot come home by themselves; help draw them the map home.

Quit looking at the mountains and focus on the Mountain Mover.

Resist the urge to fight your battles, only God has the battle

plan.

Salvation outside of Jesus is not salvation.

Society decays when nobody does something that anybody could easily do.

Some things are learned only when we sit in silence and glean from the Master's table.

Standing in the gap is really a command, not a suggestion.

The devil has no power to divide the Church so, don't help him.

The Holy Spirit is my Helper; He specializes in defeating the enemy's surprise attacks.

The Holy Spirit will never reveal anything contrary to God's word.

The world may call my illogical actions foolishness, but God calls them faith.

The world revolves around a point, and that point is not me.

There is a God, and He is not me.

There is not an extent the Lord will not go to shower me with favor.

Those waiting on the Lord are never consumed.

Those who care find a way, those who don't find an excuse.

Use your talents for God while on earth; do not take them to the grave.

Watch what you read and what you watch; the enemy's devise is to operate with fear.

We must practice our dreams if we want to get there.

Whatever God uproots, stays uprooted and forgotten forever.

Withhold love for a length of time and watch it fizzle out.

Wrestling with God is the level where miracles are born.

You are not hungry if you have a loaf of bread but don't open/eat it.

You can choose to respond to human needs by quoting the Bible or taking action.

You can gauge your friendliness by those you allow to feel comfortable around you.

You can't abide in Christ if you are not abiding in the Body of Christ.

You'll be surprised what a "Christian" in God's books looks like.

Your association reveals a lot about your character.

MUSINGS

(These gleanings are personal notes garnered during my times of reflection at different phases of my life.)

Anytime is a good time for God to interrupt me.
Counting my blessings changes my perspective of God.
How comforting to remember that my Father knows what I can carry.
I am not called to fail, because I serve the God Who knows my future.
I can't be stingy and be a Christian at the same time.
I can't have the heart of God and live in disobedience.
I choose not to be intimidated by facts; I will focus on God's truth and wait for my victory.
I don't have the leisure of entertaining excuses that will stunt my progress.
I have resolved not to eat my "bread" with my "seed".
I may not be perfect, but my God is Perfection personified.
I must love God more than my answered prayers.
I refuse to endure a life that God wants me to enjoy.
I refuse to say what I see but I choose to confess what I want.
I will be careful of what I hear so I don't act out negativity.
I will not overlook the youth; they are the church of tomorrow.
I would rather stick around to do exploits in God's kingdom.
I would rather walk with God in darkness, than walk by myself in daylight.

If God allows no more changes in my life, I will still follow Him.

If God withdraws His hand from my life, complications will arrive; I must live to avoid His withdrawal.

If I don't move when God moves, I will be left behind.

It is impossible for my expectations to be short-circuited since I serve a prayer-answering God.

It is time to acquire shameless audacity in sharing God's goodness.

Prayer: Lord, please keep a king sleepless for my sake.

May I never be the reason my heritage will not serve the Lord.

May I succeed to be an addicted giver, following the footsteps of God Who gave me Christ.

May those whose destinies are tied to mine never be disappointed!

My small efforts can go a long way and make a great difference.

Satisfaction always comes with caring about what God cares about.

The closer I am to God, the farther I am from sin.

The God of Elijah will part my River Jordan.

The most important information about me is that I am loved by God.

What garment will I take off to wash which feet?

What God has for me, no one can take from me.

Whatever I use for God is never exhausted.

When I pay it forward, I am simply obeying God.

Whenever I change, my change triggers others to change; Father let me always change for the better.
Whether I act or don't act, I positively or negatively impact something, someone, somewhere.
Why should I only shine the light on problems when I can get in the trenches and help to dig?
You can share your knowledge but you can only birth what you are.
Prayer: Father, may I be steady and let those around me borrow from my peace.

Prayer: *Father, may I never be naked before You when I "look" clothed to the world.*

GLEANINGS FROM A PRAYER TOUR

(These gleanings were gathered from my observations during a prayer tour in which I participated).

Dedicated leaders will breed dedicated followers, every time.

Healing occurs when you're busy in God's vineyard.

Keep praying even after the mountains have been leveled.

Prayer boldness arises when one goes on a prayer-tour.

Striving for the spirit of unity in the bond of peace makes for an easier and enjoyable mission.

The enemy loves to hide so he can operate. Prayer exposes, weakens and defeats him. Pray on!

The God of impossibilities can only be revealed, not explained.

The powers of darkness recognize and tremble when God's children show up to pray.

The shout of victory over our cities can change our cities' officials.

When we pray bold, audacious prayers, God surprises us with unbelievable answers.

You will always believe your prayer life is good until you encounter praying saints/giants.

JUST SHARING

(This portion of the gleanings were gathered during the Tribe's Thursday evening Bible studies)

12 Attributes Worth Acquiring

- Commitment – I have no room to put my hand to the plow and withdraw (Luke 9:62)
- Consistency – God detests lukewarmness (Revelation 3:15-16).
- Courage – I have been endowed with the spirit of power, love and a sound mind (2 Timothy 1:7)
- Faith – without it, how can I please God? (Hebrews 11:L6).
- Holiness – Without it, I can't see God (Hebrews 12:14).
- Humility – When I am humble, God is sure to lift me up (James 4:10).
- Joyfulness – It attracts people to me and keeps my heart cheerful (Proverbs 17:22).
- Love – It surpasses all other commandments (1 Corinthians 13:13).
- Obedience – It's better than sacrifice and pleases God (1 Samuel 15:22).
- Praise – That's the only way to come into God's presence (Psalm 100:4).
- Salvation – That's my entry key to Heaven (John 3:3).
- Trust – Some may trust in chariots and horses, but my trust remains in God (Psalm 20:7).

Follow Me To The Courts of My Maker

The Adonai Court: Where I pour out adoration to my "Master and Lord" (Genesis 18:3).

The El Shaddai Court: Ah! Watch and see the "Full-Breasted One" Almighty God, (Genesis 17:1) supply and nourish me in the right proportion.

The Elohim Court: "Creator God" makes creative miracles happen here. (Genesis 1:1).

The Immanuel Court: A place where the intimate "God dwells with me" (Isaiah 7:14).

The Jehovah Court: The place where "My Lord" is in charge (Exodus 6:3).

The Jehovah Jireh Court: The reason I lack nothing is because my "Provider" (Genesis 22:14) supplies my provisions here right on time.

The Jehovah Mikkadesh Court: "My Sanctifier" justifies me through the Blood of Jesus (Leviticus 20:7).

The Jehovah Nissi Court: "God My Banner" (Exodus 17:15) covers me, fights my battles, obtains the victories and I show up to praise Him.

The Jehovah Rapha Court: "My Healer" (Exodus 15:26) has

already provided me total healing at no cost to me.

The Jehovah Rohi Court: "My Shepherd" (Psalm 23:1). With Him clearing and directing my path, I cannot miss the way.

The Jehovah Shalom Court: "God my Peace" ensures my peace is whole. Complete! Nothing broken! Nothing missing! (Judges 6:24).

The Jehovah Shammah Court: (Ezekiel 48:35). His "Abiding Presence" is there wherever I am.

The Jehovah Tsidkenu Court: "My Righteousness" sees me covered in His righteousness and calls me the righteousness of God. Jeremiah (23:6).

The Tsebaoth Court: In this court, the "Lord of hosts", fights and wins my battles (1Samuel 1:3).

TO YOU, DEAR READER

Dear reader,
Thank you for taking this journey with me. You're a big part of this trip. Our journey over the gleanings does not end with the last word on the last page. Like the cow that chews, regurgitates, and chews again, let our journey of the gleanings from the Master's table begin with the last period.
Come back often. Review these gleanings often. Share them often.
Heartily,
Joy.

TYJ.

Made in the USA
Middletown, DE
30 December 2023